J
973.7
CRE

Crewe, Sabrina

The battle of Gettysburg

DEMCO

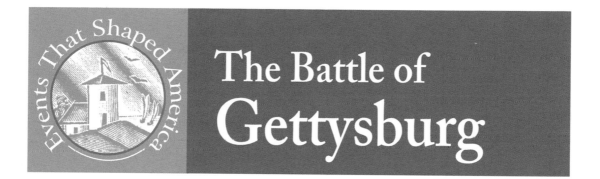

Events That Shaped America

The Battle of Gettysburg

Sabrina Crewe and Dale Anderson

Gareth Stevens Publishing

A WORLD ALMANAC EDUCATION GROUP COMPANY

Please visit our web site at: www.garethstevens.com
For a free color catalog describing Gareth Stevens Publishing's list of high-quality books and multimedia programs, call 1-800-542-2595 (USA) or 1-800-387-3178 (Canada). Gareth Stevens Publishing's fax: (414) 332-3567.

Library of Congress Cataloging-in-Publication Data

Crewe, Sabrina.
 The Battle of Gettysburg / by Sabrina Crewe and Dale Anderson.
  p. cm. — (Events that shaped America)
 Includes bibliographical references and index.
 ISBN 0-8368-3391-0 (lib. bdg.)
 1. Gettysbury, Battle of, Gettysburg, Pa., 1863—Juvenile literature. [1. Gettysburg, Battle of, Gettysburg, Pa., 1863. 2. United States—History—Civil War, 1861-1865—Campaigns.] I. Anderson, Dale, 1953- . II. Title. III. Series.
 E475.53.C93 2003
 973.7'349—dc21   2002030996

First published in 2003 by
Gareth Stevens Publishing
A World Almanac Education Group Company
330 West Olive Street, Suite 100
Milwaukee, WI 53212 USA

Produced by Discovery Books
Editor: Sabrina Crewe
Designer and page production: Sabine Beaupré
Photo researcher: Sabrina Crewe
Maps and diagrams: Stefan Chabluk
Gareth Stevens editorial direction: Mark J. Sachner
Gareth Stevens art direction: Tammy Gruenewald
Gareth Stevens production: Jessica Yanke

Photo credits: Corbis: cover, pp. 4, 6, 7, 8, 9, 10, 11, 12, 13, 16, 17, 18, 19, 21, 22, 23, 24, 25, 26, 27.

Printed in the United States of America

1 2 3 4 5 6 7 8 9 07 06 05 04 03

Contents

Introduction

About 7,000 soldiers died at Gettysburg in July 1863, approximately 4,000 on the Confederate side and 3,000 fighting for the Union.

The Blood of Brave Men

"My dead and wounded were nearly as great in number as those still on duty. They literally covered the ground. The blood stood in puddles in some places on the rocks; the ground was soaked with the blood of as brave men as ever fell on the red field of battle."

Colonel William Oates of the Confederate army, describing the fate of his men at Gettysburg in July 1863

The Battle

In the summer of 1863, two huge armies met near the small town of Gettysburg in southern Pennsylvania. They crashed into each other at the little crossroads town and battled for three days, from July 1 to July 3. Thousands of soldiers were killed, and thousands more were wounded.

The War

Even though they were fighting against each other, the two armies at Gettysburg were both American. A war in which two groups from the same country fight each other is called a civil war. The Battle of Gettysburg was part of the American Civil War, which was fought from 1861 to 1865. On one side was the **Confederate** Army, which came from the southern states (the South). On the other side was the **Union** army, which came from the northern states (the North).

After Gettysburg

Gettysburg marked a turning point in the Civil War. In the two years before the battle, the Confederate army had defeated the Union army many times. The Confederate soldiers had just begun an invasion of the North when the Battle of Gettysburg started. At Gettysburg, however, the Confederates suffered such heavy losses that they no longer posed a threat to the North.

The Cost of War

The Civil War took more lives than any American war before or since. Over 600,000 people died, not just from wounds during fighting, but from disease and while in prison camps. There is another side to the story, however. As you will see, millions of people were freed from slavery as a result of this terrible war.

In 1863, when the Battle of Gettysburg was fought, there were eleven southern states in the Confederate States of America. The rest of the states and territories remained part of the Union.

KEY
- Union states
- Confederate states
- United States territories

The Civil War Begins

Why the Civil War Started

When the United States was formed in 1776, tens of thousands of African Americans worked as slaves in the southern states. The most important part of the South's **economy** was growing cotton. Wealthy landowners had huge **plantations** that relied on the labor of many slaves to grow and pick thousands of tons of cotton.

Slavery was outlawed in northern states. By the 1850s, many in the

This slave family worked on a cotton plantation near Savannah, Georgia, in the 1860s. There were more than 3.5 million slaves in the South at the time of the Civil War.

North had become convinced that slavery was a terrible sin. Southerners, on the other hand, argued that black people were inferior to white people and therefore, they should be slaves.

A Split in the Union

Abolitionists joined the newly formed Republican Party, which aimed to stop the spread of slavery. Southerners resented this growing movement against slavery. They became even more worried when a Republican president, Abraham Lincoln, was elected in 1860. They feared that, sooner or later, they would not be allowed to keep slaves if they remained part of the United States. So, in 1861, eleven southern states left the Union and formed a new nation called the Confederate States of America. The United States of America was now split in two.

Abraham Lincoln was a Republican. He wanted to stop the spread of slavery in the United States.

The North said the South had no right to leave the Union and vowed to stop the southern states from forming their own nation. Fighting started when Confederate forces fired on the Union military post of Fort Sumter in South Carolina on April 12, 1861. The two sides formed armies, and the Civil War began.

Not only men went to war when the Civil War began. Women and their children sometimes traveled with armies, performing chores such as laundry and sewing.

Great Hopes and Grim Reality

The war opened with great hopes and high spirits on both sides. Tens of thousands of men left their homes, accompanied by cheering crowds and waving flags, to join the Confederate or Union armies. Almost everyone predicted that the war would end quickly. They were very wrong. There were four long years of battles and thousands of **casualties** before the war was over.

The War Before Gettysburg

From 1861 to 1863, Union forces won many battles that took place in western regions. Few places remained in Confederate hands. The Union army surrounded Vicksburg, Mississippi— one of the few Confederate **strongholds**—in the spring of 1863. By late June, the Confederate army inside the city was dangerously low on food and supplies.

The Emancipation Proclamation

In January 1863, President Lincoln issued a proclamation to say that all slaves in Confederate areas were freed. Lincoln's decision to declare **emancipation** changed the aim of the Civil War. Instead of being simply a struggle to reunite the nation, the Civil War was now a crusade to free millions of people from slavery as well. The news took a while to spread to blacks in the South. When it did, thousands of slaves escaped from their owners.

Meanwhile, the main armies in the war were fighting battles in eastern regions. They were the Confederate Army of Northern Virginia and the Union Army of the Potomac. The Confederate army was smaller but was doing well. Just before Gettysburg, the Confederates had won several major victories in the East.

A Declaration of Freedom
"We shout for joy that we live to recall this righteous moment. . . . 'Free forever' oh! Long enslaved millions, . . . lift up your voices with joy and thanksgiving for with freedom to the slave will come peace and safety to your country."

Frederick Douglass, abolitionist, celebrating the Emancipation Proclamation

This 1860s photograph of a Union soldier is typical of the portraits treasured by families during the Civil War.

Chapter Two
The Armies Approach

A Bold Idea

In the late spring of 1863, the Union army in the East had suffered two recent defeats. The commander of the Confederate army, Robert E. Lee, felt confident and decided to invade Pennsylvania, a northern state. There had been many battles in Virginia, a Confederate state, and Lee believed the time was right to move the battle onto Union land.

Lee wasted no time. His army was camped in northern Virginia, near the town of Fredericksburg. In early June 1863, his troops began to march north.

Robert E. Lee (1807–1870)

Robert E. Lee came from a long line of soldiers and had been an important officer in the United States Army. But when his home state of Virginia left the Union, he resigned from the U.S. Army and joined the newly formed army of his state. In May 1862, Lee was given command of the Army of Northern Virginia. He went on to become the leading Confederate commander of the Civil War. His men were devoted to him, just as he was devoted to them. He was admired by many people in the North and the South for his service during the war. After the war, Lee became president of a Virginia college.

Soldiers, often wounded, had to walk long distances from one battlefield to the next. This painting by F. D. Millet shows a Union regiment on the march.

Lee's army went west to slip behind the mountains on the eastern edge of Virginia's Shenandoah Valley. Then the army turned north and marched toward Pennsylvania. The mountains hid its movement. Within two weeks, Lee's army was in Pennsylvania. There was no exact plan. The aim of the Confederates was to cut rail lines and perhaps to capture Harrisburg, Pennsylvania's capital.

A Wretched Army

"Their dress was a wretched mixture of all cuts and colors. There was not the slightest attempt at uniformity in this respect. Every man seemed to have put on whatever he could get hold of, without regard to shape or color. . . . Their shoes, as a general thing, were poor; some of the men were entirely barefooted."

Northerner describing the Confederate army in Pennsylvania in June 1863

The Army of the Potomac traveled by foot and horseback and carried its supplies in wagons. This is a huge Army of the Potomac camp in Virginia in 1862.

A New General

Meanwhile, the Union commander, General Joe Hooker, also had his army camped by Fredericksburg. While Lee's Confederates were moving north, Hooker did nothing. President Lincoln was not pleased. He removed Hooker from command of the Army of the Potomac on June 28, 1863, replacing him with General George Gordon Meade. Since Meade was from Pennsylvania, Lincoln thought he would want to defend his home state.

Taking Charge

Upon taking charge, Meade was dismayed to find that Hooker had no plans and did not even know where all the units of the army were. Meade spent June 28 taking control and planning a march north. His aim was to protect the cities of Washington and Baltimore from any Confederate attack.

George Gordon Meade (1815–1872)

George Gordon Meade fought in the Mexican War of 1846–48 but spent most of his army career doing surveying and engineering work. When the Civil War broke out, Meade was placed in command of a brigade of Pennsylvania volunteers. From 1862 to 1863, Meade earned a reputation as a tough fighter. This is probably why Lincoln put him in charge—the president thought that the earlier commanders of his army had been too scared to fight. Meade commanded the Army of the Potomac until the end of the war and remained in the U.S. Army until his death.

Troops Reach Gettysburg

Meanwhile, Lee's move north was going well. His forces were spread out, however, when he learned that the Union army was on its way. On June 29, Lee ordered his commanders to come together at the small crossroads town of Gettysburg.

The first troops arrived at Gettysburg on June 30, 1863. A Confederate **infantry** division marched to the town from the northwest. They spotted Union **cavalry** riding up from the south and pulled back.

General John Buford was leading the Union troops. He suspected danger and sent word to the Union army coming from the south urging them to hurry.

At the Battle of Gettysburg, General Lee's army had about 75,100 soldiers ready for combat. General Meade's Union army had approximately 83,300 men. There were thousands more serving in other, non-fighting roles.

The two armies were organized along the same lines. This diagram shows the size of typical army units during the Civil War if they were complete units. The numbers in the units at Gettysburg were much smaller, however, because so many men on both sides had already been killed or wounded.

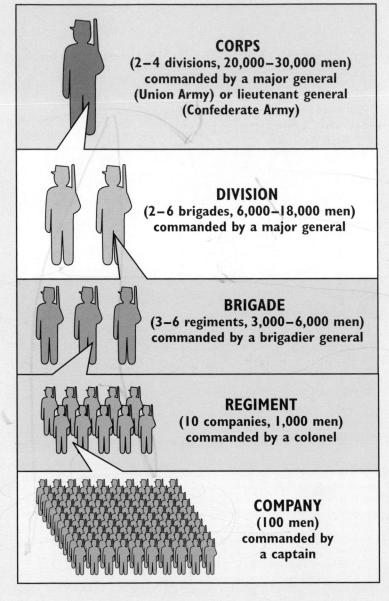

CORPS
(2–4 divisions, 20,000–30,000 men) commanded by a major general (Union Army) or lieutenant general (Confederate Army)

DIVISION
(2–6 brigades, 6,000–18,000 men) commanded by a major general

BRIGADE
(3–6 regiments, 3,000–6,000 men) commanded by a brigadier general

REGIMENT
(10 companies, 1,000 men) commanded by a colonel

COMPANY
(100 men) commanded by a captain

The Town of Gettysburg

In the 1860s, Gettysburg was a market town where farmers sold their crops and bought goods that came by wagon from eastern cities. Railroad tracks linked the town to national railroad networks. The town had several **tanneries**, many shoemakers, and shops that made wagons and carriages.

About 2,400 people lived in Gettysburg in 1863. About 200 of them were African Americans. They probably fled when the Confederate army arrived, fearing that they would be seized and sent into slavery.

The Land and the Town

A high hill called Cemetery Hill peeked above the southern edge of the town. Running south from the hill was a long rise of land called Cemetery Ridge. At its southern end were two hills, Little Round Top and Big Round Top. East of Cemetery Hill rose Culp's Hill. About a mile (1.6 kilometers) west of Cemetery Ridge was a parallel rise of land named **Seminary** Ridge. Farther west and north was another rise of land, McPherson's Ridge. These features of the landscape would play an important part in the battle that began on July 1, 1863.

This map shows the places that became important battle sites during the Battle of Gettysburg.

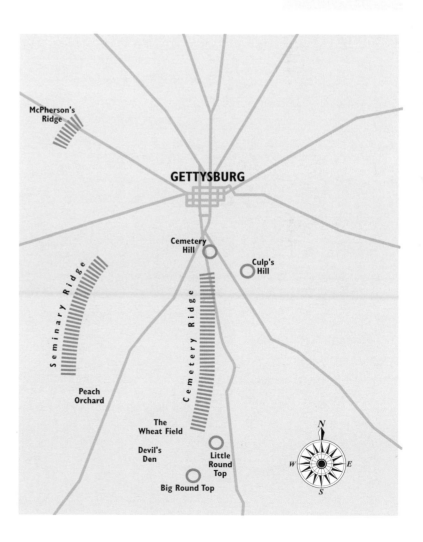

Chapter Three

The Battle

Fierce Fighting

"Up and down the **line**, men reeling and falling; splinters flying from wheels and axles where bullets hit; in rear, horses tearing and plunging, mad with wounds or terror; drivers yelling, shells bursting, shot shrieking overhead, howling about our ears or throwing up great clouds of dust where they struck; the musketry crashing on three sides of us; bullets hissing, humming and whistling everywhere. Smoke, dust, splinters, blood, wreck and carnage indescribable."

Union gunner, 4th U.S. Artillery, describing McPherson's Ridge on July 1, 1863

The First Day

On the morning of July 1, a Confederate force under General Henry Heth marched into Gettysburg. Heth's men badly needed shoes, and their commanders didn't believe the Union army was already there. But Buford's men were there, on McPherson's Ridge. They held off the Confederates for nearly two hours until **reinforcements** arrived. The Confederates retreated, but they would be back with more men.

These soldiers who died on July 1 were part of the Iron Brigade, a group of Union soldiers famous for their strength. More than 1,150 of the 1,829-man Iron Brigade were casualties after the fighting that day.

The Union Army Retreats

Other units were arriving at Gettysburg, most of them from the Confederate army. General Lee arrived, too. For much of July 1, the Union army was outnumbered by about two to one. Over hours of fighting, the Confederates managed to push the Union forces back through the town. Many men died on both sides.

By late afternoon, the Union army was in full retreat. As it turned out, however, this was not such a bad thing. By retreating, they had ended up on Cemetery Ridge, which could become a strong position. They were met there by General Winfield Scott Hancock, an important Union commander, who had just arrived. Hancock decided that Culp's Hill, Cemetery Hill, and Cemetery Ridge offered good **defensive** positions. He had the troops dig in. Through the night, more Union soldiers arrived and so did General Meade.

Why the High Ground Was Good

Generals on both sides preferred to station their troops on high ground. The higher they were placed, the better they could see an oncoming force. High ground was also easier to defend. Attacking forces had more difficulty moving uphill than on level ground. Since they advanced slowly, defenders had more time to shoot at them.

Cemetery Hill, an important high ground position for the Union army during the Battle of Gettysburg.

The fighting on Little Round Top, shown here, caused the loss of many lives on July 2. Once again, the high ground gave the Union an advantage.

The Position on Day Two

By the morning of July 2, most of Meade's army had arrived. The only missing unit was on its way, marching fast. The strong Union line was shaped like a fishhook. It included Cemetery Hill and Culp's Hill and ran the length of Cemetery Ridge.

Confederate units had also been arriving in the night. They were stretched along Seminary Ridge, opposite Cemetery Ridge and a little lower down.

Both armies knew what they needed to do. The Union army needed to hold onto their high ground. The Confederates needed to take that same ground. Only one side could succeed.

Lee Orders an Attack

General Lee ordered his men to take the hills called the Round Tops, which were south of Cemetery Ridge, and get at the Union forces that way. Luckily for the Union, General G. K. Warren of the Union army was on Little Round Top to scan the battlefield and saw the Confederates coming. He raced down the hill to find troops to defend it. After much bloody fighting, the Union soldiers finally drove the Confederates off the Round Tops.

The Wheat Field and the Peach Orchard

Some of the second day's fiercest fighting took place in the Wheat Field and in the Peach Orchard. In spite of their peaceful-sounding names, these places were filled with blood and terror on July 2. After much fighting, the Union army retreated from both sites back to Cemetery Ridge.

Field Medicine

Doctors in Civil War field hospitals did the best they could to treat the horrific wounds of warfare. But they had no way of sterilizing wounds to prevent infection. Nor did they know how to replace lost blood. Because of this, many thousands of men died after the battles were over from infected wounds or from loss of blood.

A typical Civil War field hospital, where nurses and doctors struggled to save wounded soldiers.

More Attacks

In the evening of July 2, the Confederates also attacked Culp's Hill and Cemetery Hill and dislodged the Union forces there. Twice more, however, the Confederates were forced to pull back. By dark, the Confederates had taken the Peach Orchard and Wheat Field, but Union forces had kept their high ground and gained the Round Tops, too.

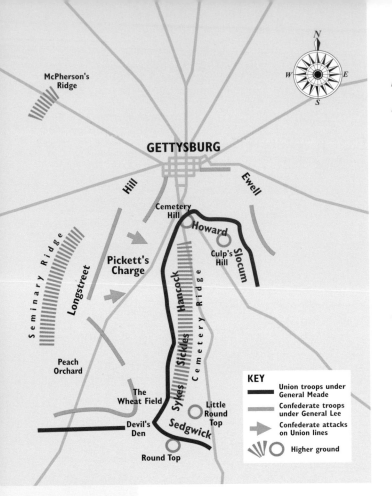

The Third Day

The next day, July 3, General Lee prepared his main attack. Pointing to Cemetery Ridge, he said, "The enemy is there, and I am going to strike him." Lee assembled nearly fifteen thousand men. But the Union line was so strong that General James Longstreet, whose men were to attack, begged his commander to think again. Lee refused to reconsider.

Pickett's Charge

Lee's attacking force had to cross nearly a mile (1.6 km) of open land from one ridge to another. They would be exposed to the deadly fire of cannons and rifles as they approached.

At about 3:00 P.M. on July 3, Major General Pickett, one of three officers commanding the attack, told Longstreet, "I shall lead my division forward, sir." As the Confederates

This map shows the positions of both armies when the Confederates charged at the Union lines on July 3.

An Impossible Task

"General, I have been a soldier all my life. I have been with soldiers engaged in fights by couples, by squads, companies, regiments, divisions, and armies, and should know, as well as anyone, what soldiers can do. It is my opinion that no 15,000 men ever arrayed for battle can take that position."

General James Longstreet, pleading with Lee to change his plan, July 3, 1863

Opposite Sides

Before the Civil War, Lewis Armistead and Winfield Scott Hancock had been best friends. But when war broke out, they took different sides. On July 3, Armistead commanded one of Pickett's brigades and Hancock was in the defending Union force. Almost immediately after reaching the Union line, Armistead was shot. Just before he died, he handed his watch to a Union officer to give to Hancock as a memento of their friendship. Hancock—himself wounded in the attack—received the watch with great sorrow.

advanced, Union cannons opened fire. The line kept moving, even as thousands of soldiers were shot down. When the attackers got closer, Union infantry began to use their rifles. Thousands more Confederates fell, but men kept coming to their deaths.

Finally, the Union fire was too much for the Confederates. Some surrendered or were captured. Most of those who survived retreated. Pickett's Charge was over, and so was the Battle of Gettysburg.

Dressed as Confederate soldiers, these men are reenacting an infantry charge in the Battle of Gettysburg.

Chapter Four

After the Battle

After the battle, both sides began the terrible task of looking among thousands of bodies for wounded survivors. Then the dead had to be buried.

The Long Road Home
"The rain fell in blinding sheets. Canvas was no protection against its fury, and the wounded men lying upon the naked boards of the wagon-bodies were drenched. Horses and mules were blinded and maddened by the wind and water. . . . [I could hear] such cries and shrieks as these: 'O God! Why can't I die?'"

General John Imboden, describing the wagons carrying the Confederate wounded back to Virginia

Lee watched the broken remnants of his army return from Pickett's Charge. "It's all my fault," he said. "It is I who have lost this fight." In the Battle of Gettysburg, the Confederate army had suffered about 28,000 casualties, including 4,000 dead. Union casualties were about 23,000, with 3,000 of those killed. Only one civilian was known to have died in the battle, when a stray bullet killed a woman named Jennie Wade in her kitchen.

The Next Day
On July 4, General Meade sent out burial parties. In the early afternoon, a heavy rain began to fall, adding to the gloom of the

22

battlefield. Lee began moving his army back to Virginia. By July 5, the Confederates had pulled out of Gettysburg and were headed south, back to Virginia.

Nursing the Wounded

Back in Gettysburg, there were thousands of wounded soldiers, including about seven thousand Confederates left behind by their army. They needed care. Much of that work in the North was carried out by the U.S. Sanitary Commission, whose volunteers gathered medicine, bandages, blankets, and clothing and sent them to the army. Nurses rushed to the battlefield at Gettysburg, as they did to the battlefields of most Civil War conflicts, to help the wounded.

The Confederacy in Ruins
"Events have succeeded one another with disastrous rapidity. . . . Yesterday we rode on the pinnacle of success—today absolute ruin seems to be our portion. The Confederacy totters to its destruction."

William Gorgas, a Confederate general, July 28, 1863

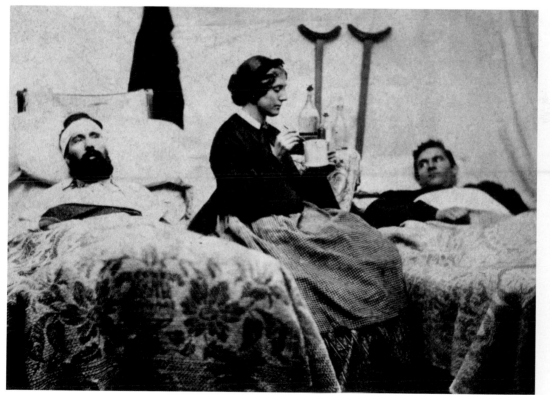

This nurse is caring for Union soldiers in a tent hospital.

On November 19, 1863, President Lincoln made a short speech at the cemetery in Gettysburg where the Union soldiers were buried. Lincoln reminded listeners that the nation had been founded in 1776 on the idea that "all men are created equal." He said that the Civil War was being fought to ensure the survival of the nation and of that idea. He praised "the brave men, living and dead" who had fought at Gettysburg.

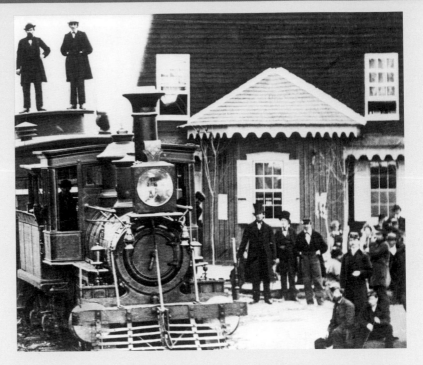

President Lincoln (center left, nearest to the engine) arrives by train to give the Gettysburg Address.

Lincoln linked the war to a larger cause, saying "It is rather for us to be here dedicated to the great task remaining before us . . . that this nation, under God, shall have a new birth of freedom—and that government of the people, by the people, and for the people, shall not perish from the earth."

The War After Gettysburg

Vicksburg fell to the Union the day after the Battle of Gettysburg ended. The tide had turned, but the war raged for two more years. Time was running out for Lee's army, however, and the Confederates grew weaker and weaker. Union commander General Ulysses S. Grant had more supplies, more weapons, and more men to throw into battle.

After the Civil War, millions of African Americans were free from slavery. They were also homeless and penniless. This is a village for "freedmen" —former slaves— in Virginia who had nowhere else to go.

The End of the Civil War

On April 9, 1865, Lee surrendered his army to Grant. Soon after, other Confederate armies surrendered, and the Civil War was over. The South would remain part of the Union, and slavery was no more. Now the United States would have to focus on rebuilding the shattered South and reuniting the divided states as a nation.

Hoping for an End

"Fondly do we hope—fervently do we pray—that this mighty **scourge** of war may speedily pass away. . . . Let us strive on to finish the work we are in; to bind up the nation's wounds; to care for him who shall have borne the battle and for his widow, and his orphan—to do all which may achieve and cherish a just and lasting peace among ourselves, and with all nations."

President Abraham Lincoln, March 4, 1865, just weeks before his fatal shooting (April 14) by assassin John Wilkes Booth

Conclusion

A statue of General Meade on horseback stands near a cannon on Cemetery Hill. From the top of the hill, visitors can look over the Gettysburg battlefield.

Gettysburg Today

Today, it doesn't look as if a terrible battle was fought at Gettysburg. The town has grown and spread in all directions. The area is full of souvenir shops and fast-food restaurants.

In 1895, the battlefield became a national park that now covers nearly 6,000 acres (2,400 hectares). It was founded to recognize the courage of the men from both sides who had fought there. Today, nearly two million people every year visit Gettysburg National Military Park.

Reminders of the Past

The cemetery holds several thousand graves, a grim reminder of the battle. Markers and monuments all over the battlefield show where key parts of the battle took place and honor the people who fought there.

The shape of the land has not changed. Visitors can look down on Cemetery Ridge from Little Round Top and realize how valuable that hill was to both sides. They can gaze from Cemetery Ridge to Seminary Ridge and wonder how so many thousands of men in Pickett's Charge could have crossed such a distance so bravely.

What Gettysburg Means to Americans

The Battle of Gettysburg was a turning point in one of the United States's biggest wars, the Civil War that brought an end to slavery. It is important for other reasons, too.

In the late 1800s, when the national park was founded, Gettysburg came to symbolize the reconciliation of North and South. The field has also come to be a symbol of peace. At the battle's anniversary in 1938, one veteran from each side dedicated a peace memorial.

Another **legacy** of Gettysburg grows from Lincoln's Gettysburg Address, which helped create the identity of the United States as a single nation. Lincoln's words also shaped people's view of what that nation stood for. The Battle of Gettysburg, like other bitter struggles in the Civil War, was fought for "a new birth of freedom."

These are graves of soldiers who died on the battlefield at Gettysburg. They have numbers rather than names because the soldiers were never identified.

1860 Abraham Lincoln is elected president of United States of America.

1861 February: Confederate States of America is formed.
April 12: Confederates fire on U.S. post Fort Sumter, beginning Civil War.

1863 January: Preliminary Emancipation Proclamation goes into effect.
Spring: Union army surrounds Confederate stronghold at Vicksburg, Mississippi.
June 3: Army of Northern Virginia begins to move north.
June 22: First Confederate infantry unit reaches Pennsylvania.
June 28: Union General George Gordon Meade is given command of Army of the Potomac.
June 29: Union army marches north under Meade's orders. Confederate commander General Robert E. Lee orders his scattered forces to meet at Gettysburg.
June 30: First forces arrive at Gettysburg.
July 1: First day of Battle of Gettysburg.
July 2: Second day of Battle of Gettysburg.
July 3: Battle of Gettysburg ends in Union victory.
July 4: Confederate army surrenders to Union army at Vicksburg.
July 5: Confederate units are gone from Gettysburg.
November 19: Lincoln delivers Gettysburg Address at dedication of Gettysburg cemetery.

1865 April 9: General Lee surrenders to General Grant, ending Civil War.
April 15: President Lincoln dies after being shot April 14 by John Wilkes Booth.

1895 National park is created at Gettysburg battlefield.

Things to Think About and Do

What Slavery Means

One condition of slavery is that slaves are not paid for their labor. Slaves, however, were also denied many of the freedoms and rights we take for granted. Find out what you can about slavery in the South before 1865. List as many things as you can find that show how slaves were denied their rights.

In the Army at Gettysburg

Imagine you are in the Union army and have just arrived at Gettysburg. Write a letter to your family telling them what it is like there: your camp and living conditions, your commanding officers and fellow soldiers, and the fighting. Tell them how you feel, describing your fears and also the beliefs that first led you to fight in the Civil War.

Pickett's Charge

Imagine you are a Confederate soldier at Gettysburg on July 3, 1863. You have been ordered to attack the Union army in Pickett's Charge. Write a journal entry describing the day of the charge.

Glossary

abolitionist:	person who supports or works toward getting rid of slavery.
casualties:	soldiers and others who are killed, wounded, missing, or captured in battle.
cavalry:	soldiers who travel and fight on horseback.
confederate:	joined together in a confederacy, which is a group of people or states united in a common cause. "Confederate" is the term used to describe soldiers fighting for the South during the Civil War.
defensive:	able to protect from attack.
economy:	system of producing and distributing goods and services.
emancipation:	freeing of enslaved African Americans.
infantry:	soldiers who travel and fight on foot.
legacy:	something left behind for future generations.
line:	arrangement of military forces in a line facing the enemy. The line represents the front of an army's territory and can push forward or be pushed back depending on who is winning.
plantation:	large farm growing cash crops.
reinforcements:	forces sent to increase the strength of a group of soldiers.
scourge:	something that causes terrible and widespread suffering.
seminary:	place of learning, particularly for people studying to be members of the clergy. Seminary Ridge was named after a seminary for Lutheran ministers that was built in Gettysburg in 1826.
stronghold:	place where a group holds out against an enemy; often used to store supplies and weapons.
tannery:	place where animal skins are treated to turn them into leather for use in shoes or other leather goods.
Union:	United States of America under a single government. "Union" is the term used for the United States during the Civil War after the southern states left; also describes soldiers fighting for the Union during the Civil War.

Further Information

Books

Bolotin, Norman. *The Civil War A to Z : A Young Reader's Guide to Over 100 People, Places, and Points of Importance.* Dutton, 2002.

Feinberg, Barbara Silberdick. *Abraham Lincoln's Gettysburg Address: Four Score and More.* Twenty-First Century Books, 2000.

Hakim, Joy. *War, Terrible War* (A History of US). Oxford University Press Children's Books, 1999.

King, David C. *Civil War Days: Discover the Past with Exciting Projects, Games, Activities, and Recipes* (American Kids in History). John Wiley, 1999.

Satern, Shelley Swanson, ed. *A Civil War Drummer Boy: The Diary of William Bircher 1861–1865.* Blue Earth Books, 2000.

Web Sites

www.civilwarhome.com/gettysbu.htm General Civil War web site with good sections and links, put together by Civil War enthusiast.

www.militaryhistoryonline.com/gettysburg/ Military history web site with enormous amount of information about Gettysburg and other Civil War battles.

www.nps.gov/gett National Park Service web site for Gettysburg National Military Park.

Useful Addresses

Gettysburg National Military Park
National Park Service
97 Taneytown Road
Gettysburg, PA 17325
Telephone: (717) 334-1124

Index

Page numbers in **bold** indicate pictures.